ASHLEY CHANDLER

THE DAYS THAT SANG MY NAME

THE DAYS THAT SANG MY NAME

POEMS BY
ASHLEY CHANDLER

The Days That Sang My Name

MILTON & HUGO L.L.C.
1001 3rd Avenue West,
Suite 430 Bradenton,
FL 34205, USA

Website: www. miltonandhugo.com
Hotline: 1- 888-778-0033
Email: info@miltonandhugo.com

Ordering Information:
Quantity sales. Special discounts are available on quantity purchases by corporations, associations, and others. For details, contact the publisher at the address above.

Library of Congress Control Number: 2025924197
ISBN-13:   979-8-89285-692-8   [Paperback Edition]
                     979-8-89285-876-2   [Hardback Edition]
                     979-8-89285-691-1   [Digital Edition]

Rev. date: 03/24/2026

To everyone who has ever searched for meaning in the
small moments of life — these poems are for you.

DEDICATION

For my family—
the ones who raised me, shaped me, and loved me into who I am.

TABLE OF CONTENTS

THE DAYS THAT SANG MY NAME

There was a time when mornings broke
With sunlit whispers through my window,
And every hour seemed to float
Like clouds that wandered soft and slow.

Barefoot summers, lemonade,
The skipping rope's bright spinning hum,
Laughter spilling through the shade,
And evenings waiting just to come.

The world was smaller, safe, and kind—
A backyard held the universe,
With secrets only trees could mind,
And magic deep in every verse.

I chased the sky with paper wings,
Found kingdoms in the mud and sand,
Believed in almost everything
And touched the stars with my own hand.

The radio sang songs to me,
The playground echoed every cheer,
And even scraped-up, skinned-up knees
Could not undo the joy that year.

My grandmother's soft call to eat,
The porch light blinking in the dark,
The way my name felt soft, complete,
As fireflies stitched light through the park.

I keep these moments close, intact—
Like shells pressed deep within my palm.
They teach me how to breathe, react,
To trust in wonder, trust in calm.

So when the world feels sharp or gray,
When time seems cold or far or strange—
I close my eyes and walk that way,
Back to the days that never change.

Back to the laughter, bright and true—
The child I was still sings in you.

THE BOND WE SHARE

For Amber

In quiet ways and louder days,
We built a world that only we could know.
Through childhood's storms and laughter's light,
Together, we learned how to grow.
Amber, in you I've always found
A place of safety, soft and kind.
Your wisdom, humor, gentle heart --
These live forever in my mind.
We share a bond no time could break,
Not distance, change, or fleeting years.

It's written deep within our hearts,
Through whispered dreams and silent tears.
We are two souls, yet somehow one,
Entwined by love, by blood, by grace.
No force on earth could pull apart
What time and life cannot replace.
So when the world feels cold or far,Know this truth, forever fair:
A sister's love stands like a light --
Unmoving. Constant. Always there.

With love, always,
[Ashley]

DYLAN, MY BRIGHT LIGHT

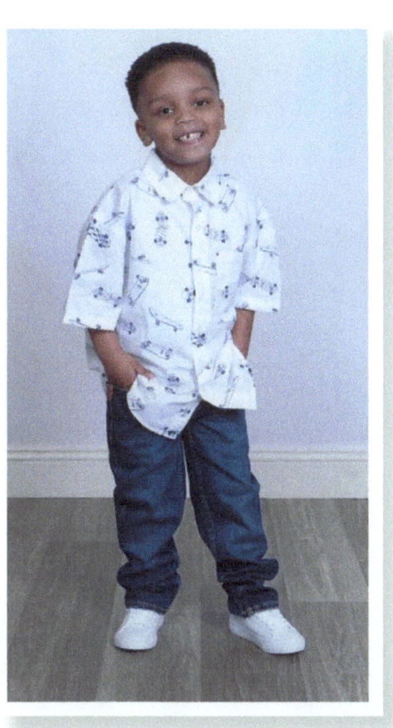

At just seven years old, you're already wise,
With wonder and laughter dancing in your eyes.
Off to Disney, we traveled with cheer,
Your silly bright spirit made magic appear.
Action figures in hand, your heroes take flight,
Imagination soaring from morning 'til night.
You call me "the best mom," my heart melts away,

Those words are my sunshine on the cloudiest day.
Your smile - oh Dylan - it lights up the air,
Like warmth in the room that's beyond all compare.
Quick with your kindness, eager to share,
Helping hands ready, always aware.
We share our own handshake, just ours to keep,
A secret between us, planted so deep.
It says, I love you, in ways words cannot,
In rhythms and claps, a love-tied knot.
My smart, silly boy, my joy and my pride,
With you in my life, love can't help but reside.
Bright as the fireworks lighting the sky,You're
my reason, my wonder, my daily why.

MY MOTHER, MY STRENGTH

Strong hands, kind heart, and a laugh so true,
There's no one in this world quite like you.
You've been my rock since my very first breath,
Guiding me forward through life's storms and tests.

Through every hard moment, you've stood by my side,
Wiping my tears when I wanted to hide.
When the world felt too heavy, you lifted me high,
Taught me to face it, to never let life pass me by.

At sixteen, Disney — a dream come to light,
Memories of laughter that still feel so bright.
And when I became a mother at only twenty-two,
You showed me with love exactly what to do.

You've given me courage, you've given me grace,
Fought every battle with strength on your face.
Made sure we had enough, though times may have been lean,
You carried it all, though it wasn't always seen.

Now when I look at the woman you are,
I see a true warrior who's traveled so far.
Proud doesn't cover the depth of my pride —
I'm blessed you're my mother, my heart, and my guide.

STILL I SHINE

I am smart, I am silly, I'm loving and brave,
Carrying laughter through the moments I save.
With joy in my heart and care in my hands,
I've learned how to grow where few understand.

I've rocked tiny babies to sleep without fear,
Watched movies alone, let my own heart cheer.
Gone shopping for treasures, both simple and sweet,
Found comfort in moments where quiet and peace meet.

But strength isn't born without battles inside,
I've carried my scars where no one could hide.
Bell's palsy young — it tried to define,
But still I stood up and said, "I will shine."

No father to lean on, no map to the way,
Still I faced every storm, every long, aching day.
There were nights when my tears spoke louder than me,
Yet somehow my heart kept fighting to be free.

Now I see courage in the mirror each night,
In the girl who kept walking, still holding on tight.
Reflective, resilient — through struggle and pain,
I bloom in the sun, and I dance in the rain.

"I STILL HEAR YOUR PAWS"

Caption: Cosmo, forever missed

The rain still taps against the glass,
Just like it did when you were here.
The house feels quiet now, too vast—
Your bark no longer fills my ear.

You'd wag your tail for treats and love,
All white, so soft, my sweet best friend.
You seemed like something sent from above,
To love us purely, to defend.

I see you still beneath my feet,
The way you'd curl up by the door.
I hear your paws—those steps so sweet—
Though they don't walk these halls no more.

You played so gentle, soft and kind,
You made cold days feel bright and new.
Your little nose would nudge, remind
Me love could live in moments, too.

Cosmo, I hope you're somewhere warm,
A place where good dogs chase and run.
Where cuddles come in gentle swarms,
And every sky holds soft, kind sun.

You gave me joy I can't explain,
You made this house feel safe, complete.
And though it hurts, though there is pain,
Your memory walks beside my feet.

At dinner time, I feel you still,
Just waiting with that wagging grace.
And in my dreams, you come—until
I wake and miss your little face.

But you're not gone—not really gone—
Your love still lives inside of me.
Your paws, your eyes, your playful yawn—
Are stitched in who I'll always be.

So run, sweet friend, and be at rest.
You were my good boy—always best.

THE WARMTH INSIDE

The rain tapped soft against the glass,
Like fingers keeping time,
While clouds pressed low and gray and thick
Beyond our little climb.
Inside the house, the lamps burned gold,
The oven hummed with heat,
And laughter drifted room to room
On quiet, slippered feet.
My mother moved with practiced hands,
The table nearly set,
While my sister joked about the rain
And how the dog was wet.
Cosmo - all white, soft and round,
With fur like winter's snow -
Came wagging, playful, friendly, proud,
And glad to let us know
He wanted cuddles, wanted treats,
And games across the floor.
He'd nudge us with his little nose,
Then circle back for more.The scent of something rich and good
Hung heavy in the air,
As coats were hung, and windows checked,
And someone fixed my hair.
I didn't know how small it was-
That house beneath the gray-
Or how these moments stitched themselves
Into my heart to stay.

I only knew the warmth inside,
The voices soft and near,
The way a family fills a space
With love enough to clear
The cold from every windowpane,
The dampness from the bone,
And leave you with the quiet truth:
You're safe. You're full. You're home.

WHEN THE MUSIC PLAYED

I didn't understand how goodbye
could sound like music.
How a song on the radio,
barely louder than a whisper,
could press against my chest
and feel like something breaking.

You were there, but already half-gone,
your breath thin as thread,
your hands folded small in your lap—
hands that had once held me steady
when the world felt too big.

The room smelled of quiet things:
old roses, faded perfume,
curtains pulled against the light.
I sat on the floor by your chair,
watching the way shadows
fell soft across your face.

The song played on—
something slow, something sad,
notes drifting like petals
through the stillness between us.
You didn't speak.
You hadn't for days.

But I listened,
as if the music might carry your voice
back from wherever it had gone—
as if the right melody
might stitch the world together again.

I didn't cry then.
I was too young to know
what tears were meant to say.
I only knew something was leaving
and I couldn't hold it in place.

After, people moved through the house
like ghosts in nice clothes,
whispering soft things I didn't understand.
But I remembered the music.
I remembered sitting quiet at your feet,
learning how love doesn't always stay,
how it sometimes leaves
in the spaces between songs.

Now, when I hear that melody—
soft, slow, broken—
I think of you.
I think of the way we said nothing
and everything
in the hush of that room.

And somewhere beneath the sadness,
I hear your voice again—
faint, warm,
telling me not to break,
even when it feels like I already have.

THE WEIGHT OF UNSAID WORDS

In this house of closed doors
and careful footsteps,
the air hums with what we've never spoken.
Words hang in corners
like pale curtains unmoved by wind,
threadbare from years of waiting.
We have learned the grammar of silence--
the hush between footsteps,
the glance that falters,
the breath held just too long.
At the table,
spoons circle in bowls
as if stirring could summon courage,
but no one speaks of the ache
threaded beneath the broth.
What was meant to be said
curled in our mouths,
turned to stone beneath our tongues,
grew roots in the darkwhere no light reached.
Still--
these walls carry the weight:
the apology unopened,
the kindness unsent,
the sorrow unnamed.
Yet somewhere beneath all this hush,

hope moves like water under ice--
quiet, steady,
waiting for the thaw.
One day, perhaps,
a hand will reach across this distance,
and words, at last,
will break like spring
from wintered ground.

A QUIET MORNING

The lights are soft,
birds are humming,
the house is quiet.
Everything feels like it's waiting,
but nothing is in a hurry.
Even my breath
moves slow.
A mug warms my hands,
steam curls like a thought
that doesn't need answering.
Outside,
leaves turn over in the breeze,
the sky stretches pale and blue.
Inside,
stillness sits with me
like an old friend.